Hello, Family Members,

Learning to read is one of the most important accomplishments of early childhood. **Hello Reader!** books are designed to help children become skilled readers who like to read. Beginning readers learn to read by remembering frequently used words like "the," "is," and "and"; by using phonics skills to decode new words; and by interpreting picture and text clues. These books provide both the stories children enjoy and the structure they need to read fluently and independently. Here are suggestions for helping your child *before*, *during*, and *after* reading:

Before
• Look at the cover and pictures and have your child predict what the story is about.
• Read the story to your child.
• Encourage your child to chime in with familiar words and phrases.
• Echo read with your child by reading a line first and having your child read it after you do.

During
• Have your child think about a word he or she does not recognize right away. Provide hints such as "Let's see if we know the sounds" and "Have we read other words like this one?"
• Encourage your child to use phonics skills to sound out new words.
• Provide the word for your child when more assistance is needed so that he or she does not struggle and the experience of reading with you is a positive one.
• Encourage your child to have fun by reading with a lot of expression . . . like an actor!

After
• Have your child keep lists of interesting and favorite words.
• Encourage your child to read the books over and over again. Have him or her read to brothers, sisters, grandparents, and even teddy bears. Repeated readings develop confidence in young readers.
• Talk about the stories. Ask and answer questions. Share ideas about the funniest and most interesting characters and events in the stories.

I do hope that you and your child enjoy this book.

—Francie Alexander
Chief Education Officer,
Scholastic Education

For Elizabeth, cat lover extraordinaire!
— M.B. and G.B.

Special thanks to Paul Sieswerda
of The Wildlife Conservation Society
for his expertise

ISBN 0-439-33408-X

Text copyright © 2002 by Melvin and Gilda Berger.

Photography credits:
Cover: Guido Alberto Rossi/The Image Bank/Getty Images; page 1 and 17 top: Ted Kerasote/Photo Researchers; page 3 and pages 18-19: Tom & Pat Leeson/Photo Researchers; pages 4-5: Francois Gohier/Photo Researchers; page 6: Muriel Nicolotti-Bios/Peter Arnold, Inc.; page 7: Fritz Polking/Peter Arnold, Inc.; pages 8-9: N.O. Tomalin/Bruce Coleman Inc.; pages 10-11: Ed Degginger/Bruce Coleman Inc.; page 12: K. Ammann/Bruce Coleman Inc.; page 13: Paul Funston/Photo Researchers; pages 14-15: Joe McDonald/Bruce Coleman Inc.; page 14 bottom: Gregory G. Dinijian/Photo Researchers; page 16 top: Martin W. Grosnick/Bruce Coleman Inc.; page 16 bottom: Lorne Sulcas/Peter Arnold, Inc.; page 17 bottom: Norman Owen Tomalin/Bruce Coleman Inc.; page 20: Tom Brakefield/Bruce Coleman Inc.; page 21: Erwin and Peggy Bauer/Bruce Coleman Inc.; pages 22-23: Renee Lynn/Photo Researchers; page 25: Tom Brakefield/Bruce Coleman Inc.; pages 26-27: Anup Shah/Dembinsky Photo Associates; page 28 top: Tom Brakefield/Bruce Coleman Inc.; page 28 bottom: Mark Newman/Photo Researchers; page 29: Anup Shah/Dembinsky Photo Associates; page 30: Manfred Danegger/Peter Arnold, Inc.; page 31: Alan & Sandy Carey/Photo Researchers; pages 32-33: F. Polking/Peter Arnold, Inc.; page 34: Mark Newman/Photo Researchers; page 35: Tim Davis/Photo Researchers; pages 36-37: Erwin and Peggy Bauer/Bruce Coleman Inc.; page 38: Tom & Pat Leeson/Photo Researchers; page 39: Tom Brakefield/Bruce Coleman Inc.; page 40: A. Visage/Peter Arnold, Inc.

Library of Congress Cataloging-in-Publication Data

Berger, Melvin.
  Grrr! : a book about big cats / by Melvin and Gilda Berger.
    p. cm. — (Hello reader! science—level 3)
    Summary: An introduction to the big cats including lions, tigers, cheetahs, jaguars, and leopards.
    ISBN: 0-439-33408-X (pbk.)
    1. Felidae—Juvenile literature. [1. Cat family (Mammals)] I. Berger, Gilda. II. Title. III. Hello science reader! Level 3.
  QL737.C23 B463 2002
  599.75—dc21

                                                                    2002003029

10 9 8 7 6 5 4   05 06

Printed in the U.S.A.
First printing, December 2002

23

GRRR!

A Book About Big Cats

by Melvin & Gilda Berger

Hello Reader! Science — Level 3

SCHOLASTIC INC. Cartwheel ·B·O·O·K·S· ®

New York Toronto London Auckland Sydney
Mexico City New Delhi Hong Kong Buenos Aires

CHAPTER 1
The World of Big Cats

Lions, **tigers**, **leopards**, **cheetahs**,
and **jaguars** are big cats.
They're a lot like small cats.
But big cats are much bigger.
And big cats do not purr.
They roar! *GRRR!*

All cats belong to the same family.
Big and small cats have 250 bones
in their bodies.
That's about 40 more bones than
you have.
The extra bones let cats twist and
bend freely.

Super-sharp eyes help make cats good
hunters.
By day, they see about as well as you do.
But at night they see much better.
Cats' eyes have a special layer.
It lets them see in very dim light.
It also makes their eyes shine in the dark.

Thirty sharp, pointed teeth help cats grab and hold the animals they hunt. These animals are called **prey**.

Every cat has five curved claws on each paw.
When they aren't using them, most cats pull their claws in.
This keeps the claws very sharp.

Did you know that cats are great sleepers?
Some rest up to 18 hours each day.
While asleep, big cats keep their tails straight out.
Small cats curl their tails around their bodies.

All cats sleep lightly.
Some even doze with one eye partly open.

CHAPTER 2
Lions: The Loudest

Of all the big cats, **lions** roar
the loudest.
GRRR!
But they do not roar to frighten prey.
Roaring helps them keep in touch
with each other.
It also helps lions warn other lions
to stay away.

Lions are very strong and powerful.
One healthy adult lion can drag a
250-pound zebra along the ground.
It would take six husky men to do
the same!

Most lions live in Africa.
A few smaller ones live
in North and South America.

African lions make their homes
on open, grassy plains.
There they can find lots
of prey to catch and eat.

Lions have brownish yellow fur
that is the color of dry grass.
The color helps lions to hide
while they hunt.
Lions mostly prey on zebras,
antelopes, wild pigs, and even
water buffalo.

The male lion has a big collar of long,
thick hair called a **mane**.
The mane makes the lion look larger
than he is.

It also protects his neck from the bites
of other male lions and enemies.

A female lion is called a **lioness**.
A lioness is usually smaller and lighter
than a male lion.
Yet, the females do most of the hunting.

The hungry lioness hunts in a special way.
She holds her body low and close
to the ground.
Quietly, she creeps toward her prey.
When near, the lioness leaps forward.
She seizes the animal with her teeth
and flings it to the ground.
Then she bites its neck.

The lioness drags the dead prey
to a shady spot.
But she does not eat it right away.

She waits until the males gather.
They feed first.

The lions rip off chunks of meat.
GULP! GULP!
They swallow huge pieces without chewing.
One lion can eat about 75 pounds of food
at a single feeding!

But lions do not eat three meals a day
the way you do.
They usually feed just once every three
or four days.

A lion and a lioness pair off
and breed when they are
about three or four years old.
The young lions are called
cubs.

At first, the cubs can't see
or walk.
But the lioness takes good
care of them.
For over a month she feeds
them milk from her body.

The mother hides her babies in safe spots.
From time to time, she changes hiding
places.
She carries the helpless cubs in her mouth,
one at a time.
After a month, she brings her cubs their
first taste of meat.

Lions are the only big cats that live
in groups.

These groups are called **prides**.

A pride can have up to 35 males, females,
and cubs.

While the lions and lionesses hunt,
the cubs play games and wrestle.
They learn to hunt by watching the adults.
The rest of the time, they sleep or rest.
Shh.

CHAPTER 3
Tigers: The Largest

Tigers are the largest
of the big cats.
Each fully grown tiger is about
nine feet long.
It can weigh over 500 pounds.
Imagine an animal longer and
heavier than a sofa!

Tigers live in Asia.
Most lions, you know, live in Africa.
So lions and tigers almost never
meet — except in zoos.

You can find tigers in every climate.

Indian tigers live in tropical rain forests.
The larger Siberian tigers live
in icy Siberia.
Other tigers live in swamps and wetlands.

Tigers like water more than the other
big cats.
In fact, they often jump into the water
the way kids do at the pool.

Tigers are great swimmers.
Sometimes they swim across rivers
to find prey.

Other times they hunt for food in the water.
But on hot, sunny days tigers might not fish
at all.
They might just paddle in the water
to keep cool.

Like other big cats, tigers catch prey
with their teeth and claws.
Tigers hunt the same animals as lions.
But tigers also eat fish, turtles, frogs,
porcupines, and monkeys.

The tiger's coat is brownish yellow
to orange, with striking black stripes.
The stripes help to hide the tiger among
trees and tall grass.
Every tiger has its own pattern of stripes.
No two patterns are alike.

Tigers mostly hunt at night.
They search out old, very young, or injured animals.
Weak prey are easier to catch than healthy animals.
Even so, tigers are able to kill only one out of every ten animals they attack!

A tiger charges its prey from behind.
It knocks the animal to the ground.
Then the tiger bites the neck to make
the kill.

Before eating, the tiger drags its victim
to a safe place.
The hiding spot is usually behind rocks,
trees, or in tall grass.
Most often, it is near water.

Here the tiger eats without fear of attack.
It tears off and swallows big pieces of meat.
The tiger leaves only the bones and stomach.
Then it takes a long drink of water — and
lies down for a nice, long nap.

One tiger eats about 50 large animals
in a year.
A mother tiger with cubs eats even more —
up to 70 animals a year!

Long ago there were lots of tigers in Asia.
But human hunters killed many of them.
Also, people built farms, houses, and roads
on tiger territory.
The tigers had few places to live and hunt.
More tigers died.

Today there are fewer than 5,000 tigers
left in the wild.
Some people protect tigers in large parks.
Others try to save tigers in zoos.
Even so, tigers are in danger
of disappearing forever.

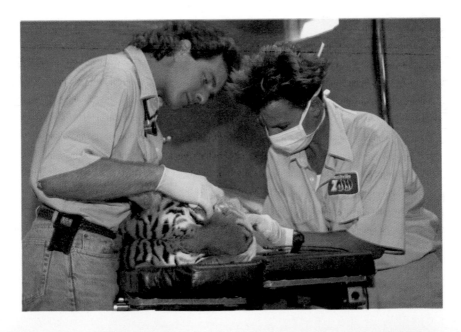

CHAPTER 4
Leopards:
The Best Climbers

Leopards make their homes
in Africa and Asia.
They hunt mainly in forests.
Excellent climbers, leopards live
both on the ground and in trees.

The coats of most leopards are
light tan with black spots.
The sun shines through the trunks
and branches of trees.
The spots make the leopards hard
to see.
This helps hide them from their prey.
It also keeps them safe
from enemy attacks.

One kind of leopard is the snow leopard.
It lives high in the mountains of Asia.
Its thick coat is light gray with brown spots.
A light-colored coat is good for hiding
in snow.

Leopards that are big and black are

sometimes
called
panthers.
Panthers
have black
spots on
black fur.
Very few panthers still live in the wild.

Leopards prey on large animals, such as monkeys, antelopes, gazelles, zebras, sheep, and goats.
They also hunt lion and cheetah cubs.

After making a kill, the leopard carries its prey up a tree.
The leopard rests the animal on a branch and starts to feed.
Other meat eaters want to share.
But none can climb as well as the leopard.

The leopard feeds slowly.

Then it stretches out on a sturdy tree branch.

You can see its paws hanging down.

Often, the leopard does not eat the whole prey.

Leopards only roar when fighting one another.

Otherwise, they bark softly.

Ten barks in a row warns other leopards
to keep away.

In leopard "talk" the barks mean, "Look out!"

Leopards in tropical
areas have babies
all year round.
In cooler areas,
leopards bear their
cubs in the spring.

The mother leopard
usually gives birth in a hole in the ground,
in a clump of bushes, or in a hollow tree trunk.
Most litters contain two or three cubs.

The newborn cubs cannot see.
Their eyes are tightly shut.
In about one week they open.
The cubs drink their mother's milk
for the first three months.
After that, the mother teaches them how
to find food.
At a year or so, the cubs are ready to hunt
for themselves.

CHAPTER 5

Cheetahs are smaller than the other
big cats.
But they can run much faster.
In fact, the cheetah is the fastest
of *all* land animals.
With its long legs and slim body,
it reaches speeds of 70 miles per hour!
That's faster than most cars on a highway!

Most cheetahs live in Africa.
At birth, young cheetahs are the size
of kittens.
The mother hides them from hyenas.
Hyenas will attack cheetah cubs that are
left alone.
A mother stays close to her cubs until
they are grown.

Like leopards, cheetahs are brownish yellow with black spots.
But cheetahs have two dark stripes that run from their eyes to their mouth.
This is a good way to tell cheetahs from leopards.

Cheetahs cannot pull in their claws like other big cats.
The claws are always out and ready to use.
They grip the ground as the cheetahs zip along.

Cheetahs can run
very fast for only
a short while.
They easily get out
of breath.
Often they do not
catch their prey
right away.

Sometimes they have to give up and rest.

Just like any other big cat, a hungry cheetah
looks for prey.
But a cheetah does not pounce on its victim.
Instead, it chases the prey.
Then a quick bite usually kills the animal.

A cheetah eats an animal very quickly.
But it rarely cleans all the meat off the bones.
Jackals and vultures wait until the cheetah
goes away.
Then they feast on the leftovers.

CHAPTER 6
Jaguars:
The Strongest

The **jaguar** looks like a leopard.
But its spots are different.
Many of the spots are rings
with black dots in the middle.
A leopard's spots do not have dots.

The jaguar is slightly larger
than a leopard.
It also has a shorter tail.
And it is more powerful.

The jaguar is the strongest big cat
in Central and South America.
It rules the jungles in this part
of the world.

No other animal will fight a jaguar. But jaguars sometimes fight each other. This happens when one jaguar tries to steal another jaguar's prey.

Until the 1900s jaguars even lived in the United States! But hunters shot many of them. Now no jaguars live in the United States or Canada.

Jaguars are forest hunters, just like leopards. They also are good climbers that often hide in trees.

And like tigers, jaguars are not afraid
of water and will swim across wide rivers.
Sometimes they catch fish there.

On land, jaguars hunt large animals,
such as deer and wild pigs.
But they also prey on small animals,
such as turtles and lizards.

All big cats are great hunters.

But sad to say, they are also widely hunted.

The big cats are becoming very rare.

Let us

- respect lions, tigers, leopards, cheetahs, and jaguars,
- get to know them better, and
- work to save them!

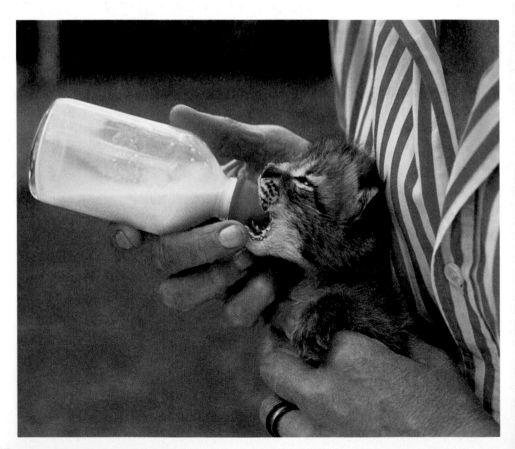